# THE LITTLE
# INSTRUCTION
# BOOK FOR
# GRANDPARENTS

THE LITTLE INSTRUCTION BOOK FOR GRANDPARENTS

An Hachette UK Company
www.hachette.co.uk

Summersdale Publishers Ltd
Part of Octopus Publishing Group Limited
Carmelite House
50 Victoria Embankment
LONDON
EC4Y 0DZ
UK

www.summersdale.com

Printed and bound in China

ISBN: 978-1-78783-571-9

Substantial discounts on bulk quantities of Summersdale books are available to corporations, professional associations and other organizations. For details contact general enquiries: telephone: +44 (0) 1243 771107 or email: enquiries@summersdale.com.

# THE LITTLE
# INSTRUCTION
# BOOK FOR
# GRANDPARENTS

MY GRANDCHILD IS BETTER THAN YOURS

**KATE FREEMAN**

ILLUSTRATIONS BY **IAN BAKER**

summersdale

Grandparents are there to help
the child get into mischief they
haven't thought of yet.

GENE PERRET

# INTRODUCTION

Ah, the joys of being a grandparent! You know already that your rose-tinted dreams of growing old gracefully and spending quality time in a comfy chair by the fire are history now, because all your spare hours are devoted to a small, sticky person, who is too irresistible – and just too damn noisy – to ignore. But who is going to teach you how to operate the over-complicated travel system, or help solve that perennial problem of how to change a loaded nappy with just one wet wipe? Because, let's be honest, things aren't what they used to be.

But don't panic! Help is at hand in the form of this little instruction book, which will guide you safely through the pitfalls and pleasures of being a grandparent and, most importantly, teach you how to keep up with the little blighters. Enjoy!

## INSTRUCTION NO.1

FROM NOW ON YOU WILL BE YOUR
GRANDCHILD'S BIGGEST FAN.

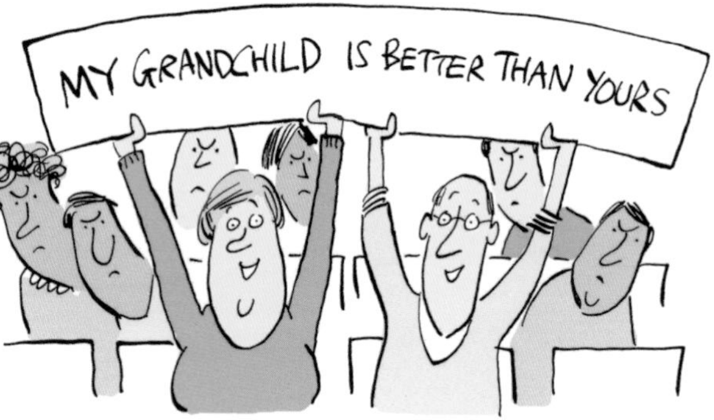
MY GRANDCHILD IS BETTER THAN YOURS

INSTRUCTION NO.2

WEAR STAIN-RESISTANT
CLOTHING AT ALL TIMES.

INSTRUCTION NO.3

ALWAYS BLAME YOUR FARTS
ON YOUR GRANDCHILD.

## INSTRUCTION NO.4

TAKE TO CALLING ANYONE YOUNGER THAN YOU "DEAR" OR "LOVE" SO YOU DON'T NEED TO WORRY ABOUT REMEMBERING ALL THOSE NAMES. IT'S EITHER THAT OR MAKING EVERYONE WEAR NAME BADGES.

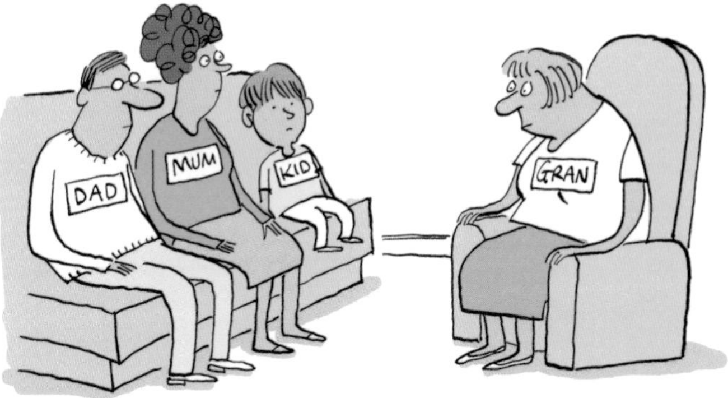
DAD
MUM
KID
GRAN

INSTRUCTION NO.5

YOU MUST ALWAYS BE IN POSSESSION OF
A LARGE NUMBER OF SWEETS. MAKE SURE
YOU NEVER RUN OUT BY STUFFING EVERY
AVAILABLE RECEPTACLE WITH CANDY.

## INSTRUCTION NO.6

### BEING ABLE TO BLAME YOUR "BAD BACK" WILL GET YOU OUT OF MANY A TRICKY SITUATION.

GLASSES AREN'T JUST BECAUSE YOUR
EYESIGHT'S STARTING TO GO – THEY'RE
PROTECTIVE EYEWEAR TOO.

INSTRUCTION NO.8

TURN YOUR CLOCKS FORWARD WHEN
THE GRANDKIDS STAY OVER TO ENSURE
AMPLE WINDING-DOWN TIME.

IF THEY'RE PARTICULARLY NOISY
WHILE YOU'RE OUT FOR A STROLL, JUST
REMARK THAT THEY ARE PRACTISING
THEIR SCALES FOR THEIR APPEARANCE
ON BABY'S GOT TALENT.

NOW YOU'RE A GRANDPARENT, THERE'S NO ESCAPING IT: PEOPLE WILL SEE YOU AS OLD AND DECREPIT. WORK THIS TO YOUR FAVOUR BY PRETENDING TO BE ASLEEP WHENEVER ANYONE NEEDS SOMETHING FROM YOU.

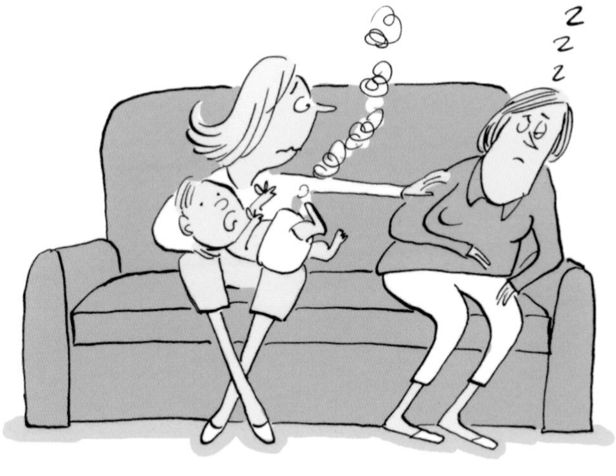
Z
Z
Z

INSTRUCTION NO.11

NEVER FALL FOR YOUR
GRANDCHILD'S LIES, NO MATTER
HOW CHERUBIC THEY LOOK.

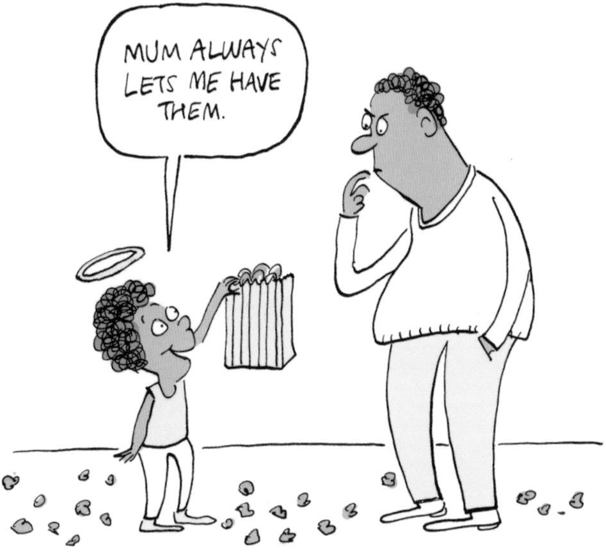
MUM ALWAYS LETS ME HAVE THEM.

REMEMBER YOUR LIMITS. YOU MIGHT
BE UP FOR THAT KICK AROUND IN
THE PARK IN THEORY, BUT YOUR
BODY MAY DISAGREE.

THAT OLD STRING VEST YOU HAVE LYING
AROUND MAKES A PERFECT CLIMBING
FRAME FOR YOUR GRANDKIDS.

USE YOUR TIME WITH YOUR GRANDKIDS
TO TEACH THEM SENSIBLE, PRACTICAL
THINGS — LIKE HOW TO TIE YOUR SHOELACES.
YOUR BACK ISN'T WHAT IT USED TO BE...

INSTRUCTION NO.15

WHEN YOU NEED A BIT OF QUIET TIME,
HIDE-AND-SEEK IS YOUR FRIEND.

INSTRUCTION NO.16

NEVER LEAVE YOUR GRANDCHILDREN
ALONE WITH THE DVD PLAYER.

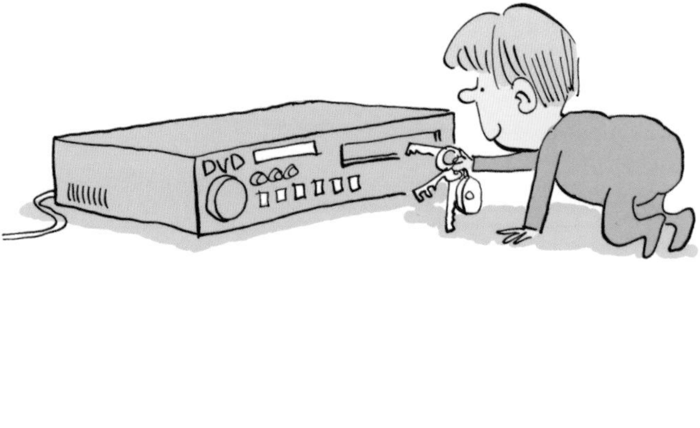
DVD

INSTRUCTION NO.17

ALWAYS CHECK YOUR SHOES
FOR SMALL TOYS BEFORE
PUTTING THEM ON.

INSTRUCTION NO.18

WHILE YOUR GRANDCHILD IS YOUNG,
YOU WILL BE THEIR FAVOURITE TOY – AND
LUCKILY GRANDPARENTS HAVE LOTS OF
INBUILT ENTERTAINMENT SYSTEMS.

INSTRUCTION NO.19

PADLOCK YOUR BISCUIT TIN.

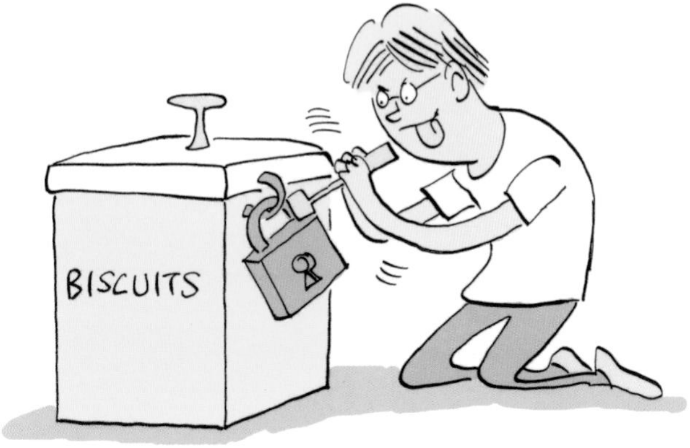
BISCUITS

INSTRUCTION NO.20

IF YOU FEEL A BIT COLD, PUT AN
EXTRA JUMPER ON YOUR GRANDCHILD.

INSIST ON HOLDING
YOUR GRANDCHILD'S HAND,
NO MATTER HOW OLD THEY ARE.

INSTRUCTION NO.22

IF YOU'RE BABYSITTING AT HOME,
GET THEM TO FIND ALL THE THINGS
YOU'VE MISLAID – SUCH AS READING
GLASSES AND SLIPPERS – BY MAKING
IT INTO A TREASURE HUNT.

TELL THE GRANDKIDS YOU DON'T HAVE ANY OF THOSE FANCY ON-DEMAND SERVICES (NETFLIX? WHAT'S THAT?), AND DEFINITELY NO CHILDREN'S CHANNELS, SO THEY MUST ALL WATCH YOUR FAVOURITE RERUNS.

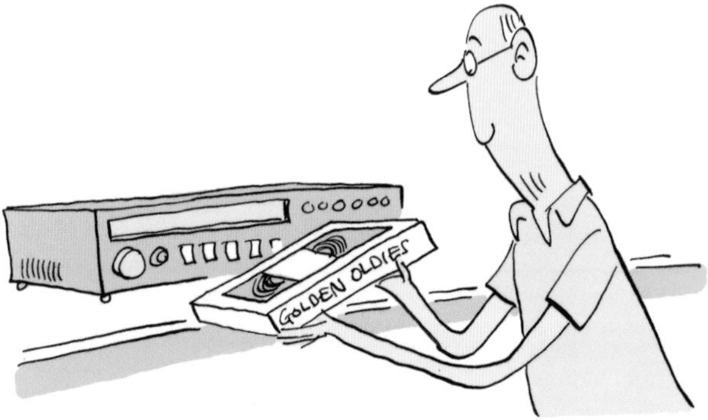
GOLDEN OLDIES

HAVING A GRANDCHILD IS A BRILLIANT
EXCUSE FOR GOING ON ALL THE
RIDES AT THE THEME PARK.

STOCK UP ON EXTRA PET TREATS
TO SOOTHE YOUR BELOVED FURRY
FRIEND AFTER THEY'VE EXPERIENCED
"THE GRANDCHILDREN".

INSTRUCTION NO.26

TELL YOUR GRANDCHILDREN ABOUT
THE MARVELLOUS EXPLOITS OF
YOUR YOUTH... EVEN IF NOT ALL
OF YOUR STORIES ARE TRUE.

TRY TO KEEP THE MANTELPIECE
FROM OVERFLOWING WITH PICTURES
OF YOUR GRANDCHILDREN.

ALL BABIES THESE DAYS ARE BORN
WITH SMARTPHONES IN THEIR HANDS,
WHICH MEANS YOU NOW HAVE FREE
TECH SUPPORT FOR LIFE.

FOOD THAT DOESN'T COME IN THE SHAPE
OF AN ANIMAL OR WITH A SMILEY FACE
ON IT IS NOT EVEN WORTH TRYING.

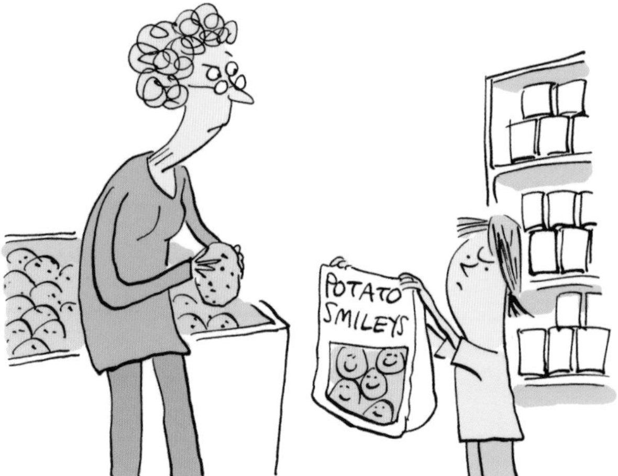
POTATO
SMILEYS

MAKE SURE TO SYNCHRONIZE YOUR
OWN AFTERNOON NAP CAREFULLY
WITH YOUR GRANDCHILDREN'S.

SEE YOUR NEW "GRANDPARENT" STATUS
AS THE PERFECT OPPORTUNITY TO REALLY
HONE THOSE KNITTING SKILLS.

OF COURSE YOUR GRANDCHILDREN ARE THE MOST ANGELIC AND ADORABLE – BUT AT LEAST HUMOUR THE OTHER GRANDPARENTS WHEN YOU ARE TALKING TO THEM AND LET THEM THINK THAT THEIRS ARE OKAY TOO.

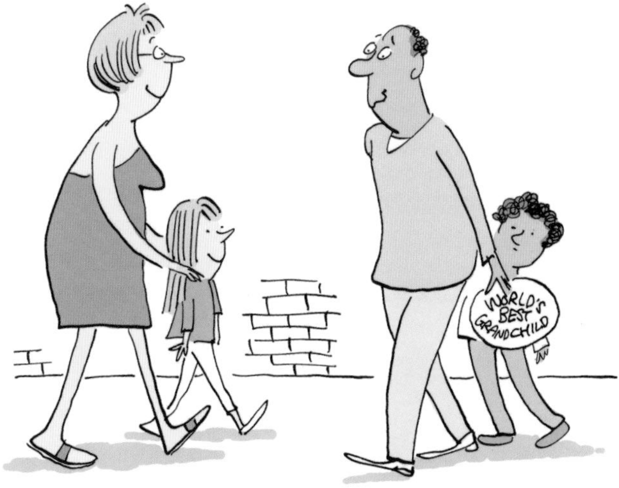
WORLD'S BEST GRANDCHILD

INSTRUCTION NO.33

THERE'S NO NEED TO BUY FANCY TOYS —
KIDS FIND CARDBOARD BOXES MUCH
MORE ENTERTAINING ANYWAY.

DON'T WORRY IF THEY REFUSE
TO GO TO SLEEP — THEY'LL WEAR
THEMSELVES OUT EVENTUALLY.

TAKE ONE LAST LOOK AT YOUR FAVOURITE
ORNAMENTS... THEN PACK THEM AWAY.
DON'T WORRY; IT'LL BE SAFE TO UNPACK
THEM AGAIN IN ROUGHLY 18 YEARS.

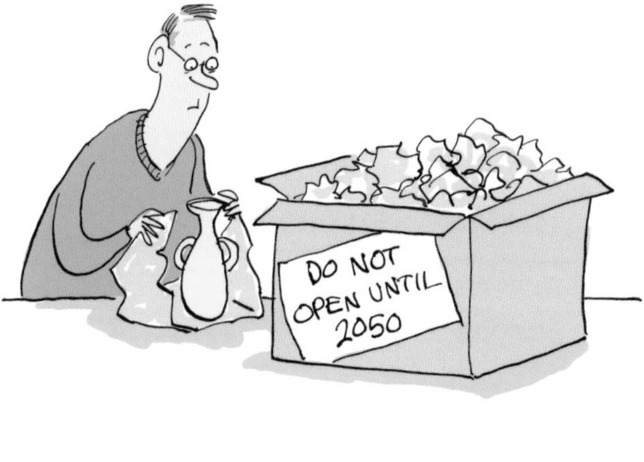
DO NOT OPEN UNTIL 2050

IT IS A TRUTH UNIVERSALLY
ACKNOWLEDGED THAT ANYTHING
YOUR GRANDCHILD MAKES IS
A WORK OF GENIUS.

SPEND AT LEAST ONE AFTERNOON A WEEK
RESEARCHING WHAT'S "IN" AND WHAT'S
"OUT" SO YOU CAN SURPRISE THE
GRANDKIDS ON THEIR NEXT VISIT.

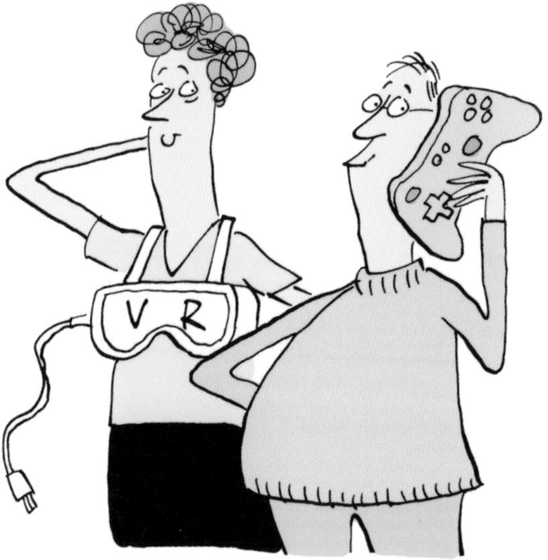
VR

INSTRUCTION NO.38

PREPARE FOR YOUR LIVING ROOM TO
BECOME THE ULTIMATE ASSAULT
COURSE/OBSTACLE RACE.

## INSTRUCTION NO.39

IF QUESTIONED, CLAIM YOUR FREQUENT
UNPLANNED NAPS ARE ACTUALLY
A FORM OF MINDFUL MEDITATION,
ESSENTIAL FOR CLEANSING YOUR
CHAKRAS. WELL, THAT'S YOUR STORY
AND YOU'RE STICKING TO IT.

IF THE GRANDKIDS ASK YOU TO
TELL THEM A SCARY STORY, TELL
THEM THAT YOU GREW UP IN A
WORLD WITHOUT SMARTPHONES,
TABLETS OR THE INTERNET.

INSTRUCTION NO.41

YOU'LL NEED TO GET USED TO
BEING COVERED IN... WAIT...
WHAT *IS* THAT?!

INSTRUCTION NO.42

ALWAYS BE SUSPICIOUS WHEN
YOUR GRANDCHILD IS QUIET.

YOU'RE NOT RESPONSIBLE FOR THEIR
LONG-TERM HEALTH, SO SUUUURE,
WHY NOT GIVE 'EM ANOTHER COOKIE?

NEVER GO TO THE PARK
STRAIGHT AFTER LUNCH.

INSTRUCTION NO.45

GIVE YOURSELF TWO DAYS
OF REST AFTER EVERY VISIT
FROM THE GRANDCHILDREN.